HEED *the* HOLLOW

HEED *the* HOLLOW

Poems

Malcolm Tariq

Winner of the Cave Canem Poetry Prize
Selected by Chris Abani

Graywolf Press

This publication is made possible, in part, by the voters of Minnesota through a Minnesota State Arts Board Operating Support grant, thanks to a legislative appropriation from the arts and cultural heritage fund. Significant support has also been provided by Target, the McKnight Foundation, the Lannan Foundation, the Amazon Literary Partnership, and other generous contributions from foundations, corporations, and individuals. To these organizations and individuals we offer our heartfelt thanks.

Published by Graywolf Press
250 Third Avenue North, Suite 600
Minneapolis, Minnesota 55401

www.graywolfpress.org

Published in the United States of America

ISBN 978-1-64445-009-3

2 4 6 8 9 7 5 3 1
First Graywolf Printing, 2019

Library of Congress Control Number: 2019931356

Cover design: Mary Austin Speaker

Cover photo: Malcolm Tariq

To the memory of

Dr. Rudolph P. Byrd
(1953–2011)

&

to each and every echo within us

Contents

III

IV

Introduction

> *"Everything I do is a love letter addressed to you."*
> —Tayari Jones, *An American Marriage*

One of the most powerful tropes that has come to mark the resplendent literature of African-Americans is the drive toward life, toward a deep celebration, toward an indefatigable love. At the heart of Black literatures is a deep desire, not just erotic, but the very essence of Eros itself, love as a new history. This is quite remarkable when one considers the difficult, painful, and unjust treatment that those of African descent have suffered and continue to suffer at the hands of the dominant culture. Black writers have never shied away from truth-telling, from an honest and unflinching engagement with the problems of racism and inequality. And yet none of these accountings have ever been couched in an unbridled rage, with a nihilism that would certainly be reasonable given the context of the work, the history that is being engaged. Of course, there has always been a double-, sometimes triple-layered struggle for certain individuals, women, and queer people. The result of centering a transformative love as the drive for the ideologies of change and art is at the core of the work of Black writers—from Phillis Wheatley, through Richard Wright and James Baldwin, and Toni Morrison, to this current time. It is an incandescent infidel poetics—all fire, all gospel, protest, lamentation, and love song, and queered against a mainstream that seeks always to appropriate, subjugate, and erase a living history that an entire people are engaged with, in reclamation. At the center of the African-American love song is the church and the gospel (liturgy, ritual, and music). This has been, if not the throbbing heart of change for the community, the pulpit for those possessed of voice, presence, and message from Martin Luther King Jr., Malcolm X, and Baldwin, most notably.

In *Heed the Hollow*, Malcolm Tariq is not only fully aware of all this history, its weight and expectation, but also is engaged in trying to carve out a space for his voice, his newer generation, to reinscribe the second and third spaces of erasure that I mentioned earlier. His opening poem, "Power Bottom," which also acts as a closing poem that has gone through a metamorphosis, begins:

> In church
> we said *Satan, get thee behind*
> and I always laughed. A demon child

Perfectly in tune with the music, with the sentiment, and yet possessed of not only dissent, but a dark-humored double entendre, the lines and the poem immediately call into question the truth of church, the lie of church, the erasure of church, and the hidden performance of queering. The "demon child," of course, refers not only to the judgment that this body receives, but also points to the traitor within, a double indictment.

But this voice is protest and something more, something akin to W. E. B. Du Bois and the idea of double consciousness, the idea that the dispossessed and othered see themselves through the eyes of their oppressors, as well as seeing themselves for who they truly are. What differs here is that the layering of selves is more complicated and asks about a self that can be doubly othered by mainstream and home alike, while simultaneously offering a choice of how this layered and conflicted and cleaved self will react to the double othering. How to subvert the old paradigm, while playing in the field of it (because, really, what other choice is there?), and without somehow centering the old while pushing against it. Language and the deployment of innuendo, allusion, humor, and other forms of subversion are at the heart of African-American literatures (hymns, gospel songs, poems, novels, etc.) and harbor languages:

Bop: Black Queer Southern Studies

Not *queer* as in strange, but *black* as in
passing it. In childhood we learned
how to be men: not to trust ourselves
was how to survive. Our bodies whet
against each other, we held tree bark by day,
tasted its sweet in the dead of night.

Not only are we witnessing a new gospel emerge, but also we are witnessing the subversion of the old. And yet the familiar tropes of passing (in the past used almost singularly to define racial constructs) are reinscribed and also subverted because this passing is gendered (passing as particular masculinities) and queered. The performing of a stereotype while a new self is honed (no accident the word "whet") from the old, with a new hope forged from a deep forgetting. Love, again. The song here, not unlike Walt Whitman's, is of an ever-reinventing self—an inscription of self as hush. In the penultimate stanza of "Bop: Black Queer Southern Studies":

Say it. Say it again: I am and I am and I am

This deep struggle is against a land, a nation, a place (which is really myth, the story a people tell of land) at once loved and despised or at least resented. The struggle to contend with the legacy of slavery and its ruination of the Black self, and the damages done to it by forced rapes of both men and women (thus its very queerness brought always into question and stained with a violence and self-loathing), and the attempt to come to an uneasy peace are worked out beautifully in these poems:

Deep Root

Consider its motherly grip, the land
that bends but never breaks us,
how the root of it bends and bends
like a crooked finger pointed at me

Anyone from a protocol-heavy culture will understand that the space between social manners and the deeper truth of a culture and self and the danger that is always present proves near impossible to mitigate:

A Woman Hangs a Cotton Boll Wreath on Her Door

and the hollow of it tightens into a collar
or a noose—decorative or death
sentence. Either way we are both caught

There is a near claustrophobic weight of history and its destructiveness and the responding and reinvention of a new twenty-first-century self that strains against the limits of state, culture, normativity, and nation. There are many places in this book where problematic and uncomfortable conflations are made between the erotics of sex and race and the beatings and the other violences of slavery and state-sanctioned actions. This love here, this Eros, covers the full gamut of expression and exploration, and while not fully covered (because what single book could?), it marks the possibility of a new set of terms to expand on the already beautifully complicated aesthetics of the grotesque (think Mikhail Bakhtin and Morrison) at play within American history.

This is where we find Malcolm Tariq's work, on the cusp of a new South, a new Black, a new self-love, a new history. He is one of a new emerging crop of writers that is redefining Blackness in the United States and that includes voices as diverse as Safia Elhillo, Mahtem Shiferraw, Danez Smith, and others too many to mention. Come read these love letters and feel this robust and non-sentimental but affirming love.

Chris Abani

HEED *the* HOLLOW

Each is intimately connected with the bottom and the extremest reach of time:

Each is composed of substances identical with the substance of all that surrounds him, both the common objects of his disregard, and the hot centers of stars:

All that each person is, and experiences, and shall never experience, in body and in mind, all these things are differing expressions of himself and of one root, and are identical: and not one of these things nor one of these persons is ever quite to be duplicated, nor replaced, nor has it ever quite had precedent: but each is a new and incommunicably tender life, wounded in every breath, and almost as hardly killed as easily wounded: sustaining, for a while, without defense, the enormous assaults of the universe:

—*James Agee*, Let Us Now Praise Famous Men

When I think of desire,
it is in the same way that I do

God: as parable, any steep
and blue water, things that are always
there, they only wait

to be sounded.

—*Carl Phillips*, "Hymn," Pastoral

Power Bottom

                    In church
we said *Satan, get thee behind*
and I always laughed. A demon child
with a twisted mouth,
at supper time I refused meat
to suck on bones. In the alley
behind the house what grew besides
berries I was told not to touch? I licked
the blood at the root. A bitter crop,
I came screaming—never tell me
to be quiet again. I know what life
the wind sucks, but what hits harder
than a hungry hand scorn by
a gallant South? I want it to try me.
Trust me, you've never felt a mouth
this sweet. This thorny. They said,
somebody put sugar in his tank;
I thought myself an army.
Commander, when I tell you to
fuck me, I don't mean
for your tree to drop in a spirit-filled
chamber of burning flesh.
I mean grow a thicker root. I mean
to say: crow, pluck me. Too much
sweetness can kill you and this
plantation can never be too used.
In the end I will have you
hung up, trapped in my Southern breeze.

I

I wondered if you thought we were lost.
We weren't lost. We were *loss*.

—*Robin Coste Lewis, "Plantation"*

Bop: Black Queer Southern Studies

Not *queer* as in strange, but *black* as in
passing it. In childhood we learned
how to be men: not to trust ourselves
was how to survive. Our bodies whet
against each other, we held tree bark by day,
tasted its sweet in the dead of night.

I believe, I believe I'll go back home,
grindin business in my hand . . .

I don't hate the South, I hate its longing to
forget ruin. I hate its calling of my not name.
It is its own, as I am also. Learned
the righteous way, I've bled bad blood
and bleed. O, mighty land, are we not the same,
made of oak, Atlantic terror, and teeth?
I don't hate the South, I hate the Southern—
its brand of voiding and voiding and voiding.

I believe, I believe I'll go back home,
grindin business in my hand . . .

Say it. Say it again: I am and I am and I am
in spite of——. What is this visceral silence
if not a coffin? A shell, be it crushed,
was once and is always a part of everything
I am leaning into—the capsule, even memories
taut, trite, and tense I ain't studyin.

I believe, I believe I'll go back home,
grindin business in my hand . . .

On Tybee Island

I heed a path trotted for me before.
I am this fragile—foraging
and foraging and foraging. What else
is there but the abandoned shells
beneath my feet that I must rescue?
At home, I place their hollow against
my own, finding once more the unforgivable
howl and sway of the ocean,
its retreat and return. In my parents' day,
I was not allowed here. Jim Crow
wagged his dry finger in our faces,
threw us inland. A child, what do
I know about boundaries and lean my tender
body inward into a shell, longing
for the promise of the shore. In the city,
they taunt me—the abandoned once more
broken carnage cradled by cement
that makes up the walls of buildings
I touch, the houses I live in. Once more
the voice held hostage in the same sidewalks
my body performs its deflecting. I turn about,
forever facing east. Forever face black,
limbs dark rolls of tidewater I've learned
to contort into obedience. When the ocean calls
me, it isn't that hard to obey. On Tybee Island
where they did not want us
splayed into the shore, I return to the site
of injury—my body this many ways
controlled. This many ways broken.
This many ways I will reclaim. Somewhere
there is always an eye for me or against.
There is my parents' aching plea to conform.

Deep Root

Consider its motherly grip, the land
that bends but never breaks us,
how the root of it bends and bends
like a crooked finger pointed at me
or from or curving inwards
both ways at once, its tiny veins
extracting its very life from soil
it now calls its own. Here I am
made into a likeness, son native to
its shape—a whip laid bare on my flesh,
homing hurt. Father, in our silence
we speak in tongues and the dirt
in my mouth crops the sweet potato,
its deep root lodged south in my throat.
Consider the fact of it is but a root itself,
the shape of it posed as a heart. However
conflicted this nation, this body: *I yam
what I am* and nothing else—.

Malcolm Tariq's Black Bottom

His Tastykake
            cake
His Doublicious Kandy Kake
            cake cake
the bounce
of his Little Debbie
            cake
subtle stretch
marks of it makes a Zebra
            cake cake
playing Hostess
for Ho Hos
no Twinkies
but Ding Dong
            cake
pound by pound
            cake cake
pounded smacked until
it's red velvet
            cake
on the serving plate
in its birthday suit
in the birthday suite
the sweet birthday
            cake cake
as wished on the Moon
Pie as wanted by teeth
tongue when upside down
            cake
feast for days
            cake cake
feast for eyes
watch it now
            cake
walk the cakewalk

call swipesy your attention
in ragtime
turn a precise corner
the fine point
ain't no cakewalk
belle of the ball
                    cake cake
walks
imitates its own trade
mark real caked
                    cake
drop
                    cake cake
this
                    cake
walks the floor
not to be judged
by the master
of the cakewalk trade
though he watch
                    cake cake
got a sweet tooth
for surprise
                    cake
wants to sponge
                    cake cake
but this
                    cake
be its own prize
snatched like a real
                    cake cake
no Devil Square
will Devil Creme
or Sno Ball
this Cocoa Creme
                    cake
will walk
brains out in form

        cake cake

be its own

you cannot take

        cake

you cannot have

        cake cake

although

you may eat it

A Woman Hangs a Cotton Boll Wreath on Her Door

and the hollow of it tightens into a collar
or a noose—decorative or death
sentence. Either way we are both caught

in the thick of this relic—
inheritance as grown and sewn
into the fabric of our lives,

omnipresent and full bodied even now
standing guard at the heavy door
to both welcome and deny me entry.

This beautiful cotton weaves all
through the black in me, the root
of what we have become

in guarding these cotton bolls. We evil
to linger in such signs. How could we
not remember, I want to

ask her of this cotton, boll weevil
I am to memory, these twigs
bound as a halo, as kin,

like a nigger hanging on watchnight.
How beautifully it lights up
these dark times, these hands

still ripe and bloody from the picking.

Niggerhead

How far into oblivion can I descend?
My mouth holds this much history,

this scorched tonguing of white flesh.
O Master! How I long to tell of it,

to be held even in this dread
locked grip of hand thrusting my past

into its future era—the next pillage
of face. Bottom. Slapped into obedience.

Is this pleasure? I want to remember
all of it—how this hide is prey.

How desire drives me into
an animal thing. I swallow

and drown into the seed of it—
the living touching the living dead.

Index to the American Slave

for whites who—somehow—have asked

Nestled among books, the spine bleeds
restraint. I attempt

my chances, finding but row upon row
of property labeled, a record
sorted by interviewer, master, narrator,
state—whose story is it?

How many ways do you find yourselves
here? Names tied to antithesis. How many ways

do I find myself? Thus far, still waiting.

And though located, not found.
The deep root clenched to dirt.
Its blood root deep but unnamable

save the stock or kin.

Let the record show: we cannot
call our names without uttering yours,
the mess of your lives stuck between our teeth.

Let the record show: we still lurk
in branches your family trees denied us,
hanging in the balance. Blood-

thirsty leaves. Cataloged
in that way—our not names.

Slave Play

                    I am searching for freedom
within this bondage. Liken it to the holy
                    spirit that caught my mother

one Sunday. As she bent to buckle
                    I fled the body that asked my own
to speak so freely and foreign.

                    Such would be my safe word
were I as daring. My body can break open
                    at will, it's the mind that cannot—

insert cuffs and I'll think shackle,
                    say whip and I'll picture a tree
carved into flesh. So why am I

                    on my knees again with hands
for a stepping stool and a mouth's
                    forum of folly

for a chalice? *This is my body,*
                    eat ye all of it. A black man
tells me to call him

                    a nigger. A white man wants
to collar train me. (See how I am both
                    the dog and bone?) Dom

I shall not want,
                    lead me beside the still
kudzu, entangle me within the loss

                    of generations.
I know who will lead me into this,
                    but who will

bring me out? O Master,

           teach me new ways to say *I want*

when the tongue is but a muscle

           flexed on which word to be

hung. Live by the word,

           the pastor tells me. I'll die by it.

If not by these feet bound one

           to the other. Command me to follow.

O God, what have I become?

Self-Portrait as George Washington's Teeth

an erasure of his last will and testament, 9 July 1799

I, Instrument
of circumstance, hold most difficult sensations

from bodily infirmities
fed by, bound by Negro

crops. Permanent provision
is alternative testimony of his attachment

to me. Trust this donation
vested in misconceptions, meaning

the pleasure of prejudice—so desirable
an object as good matter:

Public mind, pregnant Country
limits my Honourable body,

sum object I, legal alien (I, Negro), made
as evidence of desire. My private—.

My share—. The original design of my head
from me to him unsheathes blood

for unsheathed domain bounded at the Gum
to the mouth of his person. My whole

deed: two third joint uses and benefits
to the Stone and Oak of the South.

Thence, I hold all the rest and residue
of lying—desire cannot be made without

my parts: four parts—one part to each
five other parts—one to four parts,

one part each give two parts; one part
three parts: one part to each one

other part; that is—to each a third of
that part three other parts of person is

unknown to him. To take stock and repair
a new one of Brick. To remain entombed here

without oration. To digest his sense of intention.
I, binding witness of the State.

The Road to Chocolate Plantation

I

We leave Savannah in search of searching.
      My foot weighs down the road for an hour

until we cross over into Meridian—a journey
      I've taken before, not in this seat

but following my cousin's curious eye
      for history. At sixteen, I understood then

what I can't recall today. I remember
      the drive, the walk to the shore, and

the bus ride into Sapelo. I remember picking at
      a charred mullet fish fresh from the water,

roaming the heritage festival, scanning a Bible
      in Gullah—native and not. Today there is none

of that, only the deeper search of remembrance
      and belonging—capturing some stable place

between rippling gray water and shore.
      I drive further. In the back, my baby

brother's head bobs against the window—
      his first journey, already courting sleep.

II

At the port we board the school bus, its rickety
        machinery—aged but useful—carries us

into the island, past Behavior Cemetery,
        past the post office, past into another past.

The tour guide's heavy foot plunges further
        and we lurch into the dense coastal Georgia bush—

the stick-like trunks tall and fallen, the spikey
        growth of small palm trees waving us through.

Beneath us, the red earth brambles up
        after yesterday's rain, the puddles bound

to form rivers that could swallow us
        here on an island nearly lost to memory.

We trudge forward, and I see myself
        in my brother sitting across from me

as if on a school field trip, unsure
        of the destination but down for the ride.

III

At Chocolate Plantation
        I heed a path trotted for me before.

I am this studious—furthering
        and furthering and furthering. What else

is there but the tabby walls crushed
        beneath my feet, nearly forgotten?

Like me, they too were shaped by the hands
        of ancestors. Beyond, my brother

walks through and in the historical,
        not privy to the storied. At ten years old,

he looks for the shells that have fallen
        from brick, those dislodged

or never having found place in stone.
        I wonder what he will take from this

and search for narrative, placing the hollow
        against my own for a voice, a whisper, a sigh.

We explore separately, seventeen years
        between us and what we believe to know

about heritage. In the end, we each take
      what we need to survive.

On an opposite shore, I ask what he has learned.
      "That the slaves made these," he says,

holding forth his collection of fragile fossil.
      He is the smarter one, having taken narrative

into his own hands before its forgetting—
      using more than his ear for the listening.

II

You had to be in the hollow of it to taste it

You had to see how in such lack
Invention takes hold

—*Rickey Laurentiis, "I Saw I Dreamt Two Men"*

On Stone Mountain

I heed a path trotted for me before.
I am this southern—following
and following and following. What else
is there but the stone clapping
against my feet like a heartbeat—*Thy name*
I love; I love thy rocks and rills. I walk
Stone Mountain, its past ridden with scars,
the names of walkers past etched
and painted onto its surface. I scratch
my gravel. I am scorn by my will
to reach the top when at the bottom
that old flag hangs, forever willowing
in the wind, the shape of its arms forming
an *X* I have carried thus far already
as burden and haunt—home branded
onto my very back. And I cannot.
Almost there, and I cannot take that stand.
And sit near the rocks not too far
from touching the blue sky overhead,
looking out into the distant city
that I break daily as bread.
I try to look away (*look away!*),
but everywhere I am facing south.
Everywhere I face my country, my tears
of thee—*Old times there are not*
forgotten! I am afraid of what awaits me.
I am afraid of the wind that carries
and whispers and wisps.
The wind that can collect my body
and throw it against any hard thing,
into any tree, a hanging symbol
of victory etched with your name
and your name and yours. Almost there.
But I descend.

Sugar

echoing Jean Toomer
in memory of Dr. Rudolph P. Byrd

I want you to remember everything I've suffered—
cracked hands, bent back, wrought mouthful of cane
scored with sorrow songs of a slave soul.
My field hand works command: what is harvest
without the promise of more? A sea of red
my flesh will surrender. Such terror to desire sweet.

Torture me with beauty—I am the hole history of sweet.
Can't you see it? My skin, like dusk, I've suffered
to pull back; endless stretch of red
running valley deep; yielding throat; cane-
lipped scented mouth—I crave more than harvest,
the promise that God's body must have a soul.

Black isn't made to live; my body is opaque to the soul.
Is boundless bounty of muscadine, scuppernong, sweet-
gum, honeysuckle, pine—I am every man's harvest.
Each one has entered a sticky field and suffered
a failure to leave. Has opened his throat to cane
stalk. Has gotten lost feasting deep in the red.

Who says God would not dare suck black red
blood? Black—magnetically so—midnight's soul—
towering majestic black bodies of ripe cane—
black reapers swinging scythes sharpened for sweet
conquest—black balanced and pulled against to suffer
pure sugar as subtlety—black turning a white harvest.

An orgy for some genius of the South, this harvest.
I dance as the tongues of flames of a red-
burning moon. Even my blood has suffered:
one uncle died of diabetes, another a queer soul
with too much sugar—a cup runneth over in sweet.
Listen: I am nothing but wind whistling in cane.

And me, I am nothing but this dark field of cane.
And me, I am the reaper weeping at harvest.
And me, even my pain is beautiful and sweet.
And me, my throat opens wide to be read.
And me, my mind too is opaque to the soul.
And me—heaving, ephemeral flesh—I suffer.

Niggerhead

How far into oblivion can it descend?
Not the head, but the holder—

he who keeps as relic my scorched
tongue. O! How I long to tell of it,

forget the ornate vestibule
in which it stands. This one season

or the next. Hand. Ear. Foot.
Breast sawed off in plunder.

Is it the body's part or the human's,
this arcade of Americana?

We pillage into the next era
unbothered by the road, its dust

settling into our skin cells—
the dead touching the dead living.

Callie Barr's Black Bottom

You may find her behind

    Rowan Oak, a shadow

        of fortress where then now

    you find no real entry place.

Where then now a tree grows

    near that door, purple flower

        heads peeking through into

    the world she left behind.

Here then now she found a home

    as shadow, covering

        it all with her big black

    small frame of big womanness

now then where the cabin creaks.

    You may find somewhere

        her portrait stuck to a wall

    where then now she lingers,

shadows peeking over her face

    to find the proclaimed Mammy

        joy. They leave themselves to

    tell her story, to guess her

age unknown and rounded out.

    Here then now she lies absent,

        erased by the very word—

    entry marked into the bottom

of history where then now

    we find no shadow of life

        as told by her. History carries

    her tale through his and her mouth.

Say: *I heard it like this*

    now then where she lingers

        on tongues that spit out the bad

    taste to tell a good story.

Say: *Here lies Mammy, born*

    in bondage, died in devotion

        and love. Where then now

    they opened earth's

mouth ready to receive her

    body. Stretched that back

        over her. Placed the tombstone

    as muzzle that says: "Mammy.

Her white children bless her,"

    where then now her black children

        listened and watched that doing,

    going back into their shadows

after she lay buried in the maid's

    uniform as they say she requested.

        Then now there was it

    emblem of her service or her life?

Where then now is Callie?

Grandma's Black Bottom

When I position the recorder, she straightens
into narrative—every inch of lived detail gone
asunder. She leans forward looking back.
I attend inquiry as I've done for years,
converging on craft. What she refuses
to say haunts this entire process of returning.
Together we construct memory: *this the bottom*,
she says, indicating this porch. This street.
This same spot that borned her mother shaped me
my mother and her billowing in the same space
for nearly a century that claimed us cost us
our lives where we make our living our business.
What we don't say is divided as communion;
it creeps along the edge of the storied.
And though I hunger for testimony, I have learned
to listen and ask later for what will never come.
What lingers in her request to not talk about
her childhood. She still remembers
to forget that. Everyone wants the strong black woman
with Sunday greens. No one wants to hear about
the dirt she washed from them, the strain that went
into the pot used in defense. Everyone wants
the black woman loud-mouthed and big but no one wants
to live in her loud-spaced silence narratives.
The dissonance dancing around them.
Everyone wants pot likker but no one wants to cleave
leaf from stem to salt the earth to dig into dirt
toward the deep root. Silence is testimony.
I take that as daily bread when she says
I didn't say anything for a long time.
This is hard to imagine, for years we slid
along walls and waited out the shrill profane of
grandma's black bottom. Her device against control.
Perhaps this is the lesson: to say what I have to
when I don't have to listen to what I'm told.

I am this obedient a grandson—listening
and listening and listening. To who else
do I owe that much? We long for stories
we aren't prepared to carry.
Foolish of me—learned negro—to feign scholarly
with this conscious backwardness. Grandma speaks
into the air waxed on repeat. Her eyes
on my steady moving pen, my forward glance.

The Body Politic

Say this isn't the whole of it,
    this frail book and its sentence.
Somebody's too-good and no-good
    grin. Somebody's God-awful

and too-full mouth. Somebody's
    tired. Somebody rattles
the cage another will die under.
    Somebody's sickle and somebody's

cell. Somebody be out they cotton-
    picking mind, somebody's else
be all up in it. I mean the weight
    of a dime in my hand before

collection. I'm talking Sunday
    be somebody's lifeline. Somebody's prison,
whose body's a pipeline?
    Teacher's judgment against

my house collateral. I'm counting
    books and lives, putting money
on books and bailouts.
    Despite this black

president, I'm thinking slum
    lords and thug porn. Family
courting the law while yo mama
    so fat and somebody's big

black _____. Three-fifths
    a body's sum. Body's worth
in inches. Whose back a bridge?
    Whose broken daddy's back

on crack? Somebody stepped
    on the beat. We dug it. A body
was bodied while politicking.
    Who done it? Somebody's

well-meaning and good intentions.
    Somebody's every day and everybody.
(You love somebody's lost.)
    Nobody's somebody you can't give back—

somebody's something paid for it.
    Somebody's womb be somebody's
gun. Somebody's baby
    against bullet. The plot quickens.

Headstone-bodied bodies
    be bodying days. Centuries
bookend the dash. Our lives
    will fit within it. Our lives will

abandon the boundaries of the body,
    the way some bodies belong to
the state. I stay stating my name
    like it matters: *I am* and *I am*

                    and *I am*—.

Drapetomania

forgive the swamp its magic   niggers
and mischief to grab onto them   who flee
in the crook of its mouth and   wait
one death for another   for whispers
to become rooted in miles of muck   to run
from the crocodile's teeth but never   back
to the crack of whips here   in waters
housing the thickness of death   and birth
entangled in ropes of smog   themselves
choosing to brave the swamp to bring back
desire sick with the will to return   to life

1 Yearning

an erasure of reports compiled in Ralph Ginzburg's 100 Years of Lynchings *(1962)*

the first negro
history was taken from bed
gagged bound and received a riding
over a little white mob
fully handed seized picked up
rushed and made for torture
noble country labor

surround the small sapling
fasten and watch
eat his flesh
his body witness
the contortions of his extreme
agony his fiendish deeds
with unfeigning satisfaction

blood was left
to tell the story the bone
snatched by people who fought
over the body seeking one
possessed occasion
only murmur
was plunged into his flesh

believe it the first lick
at his feet the crowd was satisfied
with the play of no secrecy
seeing the head pinned

the anal savage
the exhibition
the world
the state
the best devil man
the spectacle
the flesh
the bones history makes
the fact

the nation
the thousands
the centuries
the naked
the primitive man
the victim
the religious
the desperate position
the great work

the rise
the quiverings
the writhings of the frame
the jostling

      the negro loosens
      the upper part of his body

the relish of oil
      and at last comes
the man's release

the spread of what is left of a confession
the mob boasts
      more savage

not one hand nor a single voice
instead the shrieking boy
the crowd cheered in piping

every act was done in the open
from one end, peculiar assault
a beautiful ramified
hardened determination
of the Lash

the mob pulled slowly
into both sides jostled roughly
against demand
for the prisoner bold movement
swiftly with no panic

the number swelled
from a struggle to come
by force

ropes loosely attached
to whip his head and feet

strapped against the tree
large quantities of bush
and larger bits of oil poured
while he was praying for speed

his clothing one man had
in his hand filled almost bursting
from his head again
and again the stained trousers

in ecstasy a neighbor
pounced upon him

and made him promise not to
be too quick

eager hands reach waist
long poles to push
in an upright position
again and again

the crowd feeding
the Lash

to wood flesh said
"I touched his doom
as all that may follow"

rendered hands feel
as if they could walk the loneliest
molested black man

Lash
Lash
Lash

groaning

Lash
Lash
Lash

swung over an oak
he was the tree
the limb the limb
the rope hoisted
the dangling limb of a tree
grew out of one color

white

face down

for two hours the crowd came
and went he was passed
around several times

a boy continued asking for bids

uttering ass

a large posse quickly
bound hand and foot

the negro broke

in the spirit of the affair
he said inflict me

a fair request was granted
the people ordered

the negro faggot
laid and driven deep

two white girls whipped
the negro with a barbed wire
and brass knuckles

the ass worn out
for a white family

Dick to revenge Dick

each ass waiting for white men
to use a train of Dick

the rendered Dick
the bullet a Confederate law

an ungodly crime

the same hideous people
jerking him off
silence him

the race of white men
blow him hammer his
mouth and unsex him

then twelve masked men red
hot with his broken black body
rush the lower part of his business
they spit in his face hanging limp

the spectator female spits
in his face begging to give a hand
and eat him all night

the negro showed his number
while the white men ate leisurely
and looked on while he inch
by inch began to swallow
two men who lick his chest and face

after riding for several hours
both men pulled out and ordered the colored
man to dance

three colored men were tied
to a huge flank
every inch of the bottoms beaten

the sheriff said to them
BE GOOD

an orgy of erect white men
shoved the hole
fastened the rear of the body
piled fists into the negro district

white men curious about abolition

in the wildest orgy
3,000 men powered a negro
tossed the loose body in the centre
men packed so thickly
watched his spread surrender to them

armed with desire
continually leaping on the negro
presence all the clothes torn
and he hung nude

a white man beat my rear
in the canefield

lowered my pants and beating me
he said

how it feel

Nocturne: Without Sanctuary

after Ken Gonzales-Day

A man points me into a dark sky.
I look up to emptiness, lost
already to his wonder
gaze for girth before the drop
of clothing, caress of the neck, broken
silence of air leaving this mouth.
Bed as my witness, I come
as Tragedy. Fantasy. Film
Noir in one short act.
Only the tree will outlive it,
can tell the story as no one does,
will utter *passion* and mean
possession, will say *fire*
and mean *desire*. I want
to unlearn this body, forgive
the spectacle it is. *Gallowed
be thy name*. I will take it
into antiquity. He's never had
a black man. I've never had myself.
I want to imagine a world in which
I am present. Dear shadowland, say that
the cockring is not the noose. Say that
the phallus is not the faggot.

Malcolm Tariq's Black Bottom

We called it the twerk room, and dimmed lights
at house parties to grind our bodies against walls
and each other. We are two black

boys in Michigan—Georgia and Mississippi
spiraling slowly. There are names for people like us
and we live into them. My ass fits perfectly in

the seat of his person, speaks to the air between us
where I feel him rise and reach. Now his legs
guide us into the familiar;

we bend into the blade of a scythe. Outside,
our ancestors are folding fields, grinding
to heel-toe seed into the ground, their feet

drilling new life, bodies bent in heat to clap the earth,
up and down, black bottoms wading in air,
a feast for house eyes. We slow drag in a dark room

while they build a house bottom to top,
making their own cabins bend into home. They wait
at the back of the house, no room to make themselves

in rooms they made themselves. I reach for a man
under blue light, my feet planted as stone, my hands
on my thighs. He eyes a bottom bending its weight

to balance us both as the walls around us come down.
And if my people built the house, I place it in the homely
arch in the small of my back and shake what I am given.

Self-Portrait as an Unmarked Grave

Do not seek the stone without the story,
but even it cannot fit this hollow. And flesh,
flesh shall not fail me. From here,
cartilage, collagen, calcium whispers
my dissent. Witness what I've made of ruin.
To our kind, death is no descending. Each year
bramble thick with thorn advances
its assault. I rise. My dead—. My living
spill above the earth, push through blood
soil until you are made to stalk. Balance
in cruel wind. Tangle of limbs
brown scar the landscape. Roots refuse
to manumit my bone. We monument.
Carry that in your descendant order—
no longer gentle, but violent bush
evergreening deep in winter's scorn.

On Sullivan's Island

I heed a path trotted for me before.
I am this impaired—forgetting
and forgetting and forgetting. What else
is this wave crashing into shore
but an attempt to cleave remembrance?
Overhead, the dark sky engulfs
the Low Country, once welcome spot
and terror for the ancestors, always
a nest for the captors. Now,
baby strollers and casual dog walks
file before a single marquee meant to hold
place for history—leisure where once labor.
What work have I come here to do
besides witness? I go from shore to shore
seeking clarity, to stand on the threshold
of past and present where land and sea
court death. I search my mind for what remains
of generational sanity. There is nothing
but bondage. Ahead, the sign reads:
"Deadly currents, deep holes"
and forbids the swim out. I could chase
the distance with salt. I could run
face forward into what has already claimed me
without regret. This ocean swallows
the whole of me. I could join it
or become another buoy signaling lost.

III

. . . who ever heard of a Southerner getting on
his knees to any Yankee, or anyone.

—Jean Toomer, "Blood Burning Moon"

Fucking [with] Ralph Ellison

My home is my hole
is warm and full of light. Tight
muscles, clenched fist. You feel me?
You see me? Invisible, haint.
Flesh and bone. Fiber and liquids.
My hole, my homey hole
ain't cold like no grave but the dead
do sleep here. They is home
to my hole like me—real and unreal.
Seen and unseen. Always coiled
into myself so not to wake the dead
lest they see my hole, our home,
the in and out of there—a dark thing
always coming at you. My hole,
my home, my bottom
ground at being, seeing. You feel me?
Here we is most alive. You try
to break the distorting glass
but the mirror still looks back at us
in the darkness of light. I am
ain't no spook but and I
sure do fight one without it me
knowing. Put your fist in mine, I won't
deny it. Deny you. Brothers
and sisters: my sex this morning is
the blackness of blackness most black.

Fucking : A : Proclamation

What if the ancestors are watching us fuck?
I wouldn't mind their inspection—my aunt's
doubled-over laughter at your hand's lock
on my ass I've come this far to surrender,
witness to the crashing of our bodies.
And if she is smoking she passes the joint
to a grandmother whose neck is clasped tightly
by the missus, flinging in rhythm to
our swinging, still sucking and blowing
the smoke into our faces. Be they privy
and proud of what our tongues have made
of lashing, how they've learned to call
fleshly desire into the living. We fight
and call it want. Your hands bury
me as a matter of need. For coming
this close to death is our own doing and undoing.
The ancestors are watching us fuck and
I'm holding your back's unmarked smooth,
my mind still a scatter. For the man
has told us we're no good for anything
but fucking. Our bodies are material
interests: the wood frame balancing another,
the paper map marking so many journeys
but our own. Called brute, savage, boy—
we suck dicks, but they are hard
to swallow. Every bit is but a sight of terror—
the rope kissing the neck, embracing
the ankles, the wrists, my mouth
stuffed with your fingers tasting of blood
is but for how I choose to undo——.
How to fuck in spite of——? When you shoot,
there I am and so is the uncle's uncle
or baby mama or daddy's head
knocked up by the master's pistol—
cock cracking cranium. O!

The faces I've pillowed and long to
forget. The ancestors fucked between tabby
walls left to ruin, on dirt floors they fumbled,
leaving seed inside the earth's bottom.
Lover, we are furious flowers and just
as brutally I'd ride a dick to save my life's joy.
And if the ancestors are watching on this night,
they've praised this willful bottom. They've clapped
in rhythm to the headboard. They've stomped
with every crescendo caught gasping for air.
For finally this body is open. And this
body, it is mine.

Heed the Hollow

I want to remember everything
that has happened to me—
history of my flesh, scar of her miscarriage.
I take my own pills as I once learned
to sign for my mother's birth
control. Preventative measures.
I am learning to reproduce myself
with the shape of my mouth's consuming.
I'll swallow everything—I have to
forget to live the way men read
labels as invitations. I've heard
women in my family talk of assault
as I've heard men
talk of assaulting. I'll be something
to someone someday or nothing but
spill. Truth be told,
I want to be the last side effect
and the disease. I'll settle for
a curse. I am trying to remember
to forget the colonizer's name on
my medical chart, scripting my back.
I straighten into narrative
and carry it in spite of

my name, how he grabs me

as if prescribed. I want to forget

the way he's had me over the counter

taking him. The way he told me,

You were almost a power bottom.

Malcolm Tariq's Black Bottom

You want me to talk back to you.
I allow flesh its function—I am a body
tied to a body tied to addendum.
An arched back, a split tongue,
a sunken throat. I am a fiend
and a freak and a fuck.
I am and I am and I am
not this singular being. I am legion,
millennia of continued thrashing,
interval of wisped memory,
palm-rolled heritage. You want
a voice, a command, an avowal.
Take this moan as historical rendering,
my downward-facing sigh. *Thy rod
and thy staff they come for me.*
Soon, I may be nothing to you,
and just as I try to live with that, I find
the crown of cowrie upon my head
as thick as the leash around my neck.
You thrust your life into me and watch
it bounce back. My body releases
ten thousand tongues as you graze
walls etched with languages
of twelve centuries. They spill onto
your bare chest, waiting for an answer.
Get lost in this echo, disappear
in your hands controlling
rhythm, your mouth whispering
to a red moon. When I look back at it,
toss your name back into me.

Common Feast

To anyone, I'd tell
how the women of my family cleaned
the innards of pigs in the same way I've prepared
for a man to enter me. Both of us—

pig part and human—doused into water
as baptism or with prayer, meant to soak,
to be inspected. Meant to be pulled apart,

made ready to eat, for the mouth's
bare desire of musical flesh, muscle, tissue.

And to someone familiar, I'd recount
the process of the feast, the stewing,
the pungent scent of intestine engulfing
the afternoon air, taking hostage
our noses for what later soothed the tongue's
wanting. From this I know that

intimacy is not a clean thing;
it is difficult like this—covert
and common. Bare, as it should be:
someone says I want the mess in you
and you give it to them.

And to no one, I'd confess
that when I give myself to a man, it is rarely
the whole self in the way that it is a whole
body giving into want. At times, I have been

the silky morsel of pork waiting before the mouth.
I have been hunted, given into pursuit
to be made a whole person in need of hunger.
I've wanted to be felt this badly. I've wanted

to feel something this bad. Intimacy is that
clenched between two cheeks. Both the said
and unsaid. In the middle of the feast

we wonder if this shit is real.

Learning to Bottom

I

The last time I was called a nigger
was in a bar in East Atlanta,
where all the white people are
moving now, past 1 a.m. and three drinks
seated next to a man this many years
my senior. Having shared so many laughs
despite the space between us at a counter
once antithesis, I rise—a colored man
with painted fingernails—and hear the word
shake my hand extended in gracious departing.
I take in the entire room, my body turning
all shades of black, and think about my mother
who still prays for my safety on election nights.
I decide it's best to turn my shell inward
with the life I still possessed. My fist is a stone
in my pocket, my palm is wet with tears.
I am not home, but think to go back inside
when I see my stranger stumble outside
with an accomplice and drunkenly laugh,
"Jerry, I've upset a drag queen."

II

With his finger still inside of me,
I think *race mixing* and want
to tell him that my aunt once said
I would integrate the family, but don't
for fear of flight. Keep your name,
I will explain, I want a man big enough
to palm my hollow—an impossible
shell. *Race mixing*, I finally say and laugh
as his face turns to stone. I realize now

he thought I had found him out. I did
not, but joined our hands into a fist
on the bare floor of his small home
while he kissed my black. Years later,
I will want to ask him: which n-word
was I then—*nothing* or *never*?

III

An older gentleman walks into me.
Excuse me, sir, he says. I smile,
continue my tour of the museum.
Alone in folk art, I laugh
at my new name. Around the room,
Harold Finster's pale and pink-faced
men line the walls. We are all home,
but only one black. *Sir*, I think.
Negro, they correct. Even on paper
bodies dressed for Palm Sunday,
race is a shell projected as a stone.
Southern—*American*—heritage is this
scripture I've fingered for years,
a beloved I continue to fist.

IV

Then I came alive
as you smothered me—
body so stained with sweat that
it is nothing but tidewater.
Crush my shell into black ash,
mix me to stone in your fist
to finger. *Yes, nigga*, into my ear
you pray. I will be that. All along
I've been waiting to be called
into our name and live there.

I've let something broken
inside of me before and did not die.
Remind me we are not ruin, but stone
against sin. The ancestors have
already built our home. Palm the soft
small of my back and enter it.

Addendum

I

It was cotton that caught my eye in Brooklyn, bales of it piled on the sidewalk
lighting up the cold night, fresh and white with boll and bits of brown twigs
still stuck in it. Cotton, I thought it was. But then, snow, soft and lush
to my Southern eye. How foolish of me, I thought as I continued down

the street to the market. Returning to the benefit party thrown by the nonprofit
where I worked, I stood in the corner eyeing the group of people, some near my age,
being spoken to about programs that kept the convicted at home instead of prison.
In this room I'm one sight—brown twig among fiber—against the whites invited

to open their wallets to our cause. My face is as young and male and black
as most of our clients. Here, I could be one of them. I stand in the back
still stuck on being asked to go out in this weather to retrieve a serving tray.
The host introduces me as the guy in the back he feels bad about having to ask

to go out again, who helped make all of this possible. Suddenly, I'm the help,
despite my actual position, the degrees, the awards, the dissertation.
The next day my supervisor informs me I could count the five additional hours
I stood at the party toward the week, that I did not have to give them to the work.

In that moment, I realized he actually didn't know who I was either, because why
would I donate my time to a job for which I am underpaid and overqualified,
even more so than him? I wanted to ask this, but before I could his pale face split
open and fiber burst through boll. I wanted to pull—to pull my mind back from it.

II

Try if you can to pull your mind away from it. In Mississippi, I ask my driver
what grew in the vast green fields we were passing on our way to the airport.
He listed a few vegetables, then said, "And some of it is actually cotton,"
as if he didn't expect me to believe it. And why not? Like me, he was

a black man, a few years younger. Maybe he didn't know that I too was
Southern crop. We continued our recognition by not recognizing
how I changed the subject, that I did not want us to be two black men
on a Mississippi road talking about cotton and slave labor as if it was

so far removed from us. Looking out of the window, suddenly I remembered
that in fifth grade, a small bag of cotton was passed around the classroom
fresh from the field. Our teachers, all black, looked on as the room of black kids
with wide eyes considered the relic. We wanted to touch it, this history.

The teachers confirmed what we thought we had known, that we didn't know
about such crop, about such labor—we were too city. They used our awe to teach
a lesson: the terror of slavery, picking cotton is something we would never know,
and this is why we should behave, they sneered, heeding only our bad behavior.

They didn't tell us how history is never so much the past as it is a condition
that follows us, how already our minds were made to hull. *Actually cotton.*
I want to pull my mind away from it, but who would I be then with no history,
with no way of knowing the difference, the likeness between flesh and fiber.

Cento in Which the Narrative Precedes the Lyric

I wanted to craft a cento made from lines of slave narratives.

A cento is a poem composed from the lines of other poems.

The slave narrative is an account of bondage as told by the enslaved or the formerly enslaved.

The enslaved and the formerly enslaved, in this case, are those generations of Africans and their descendants subjected to unpaid labor, physical abuse, mental abuse, sexual abuse and exploitation, and socioeconomic disenfranchisement in the Americas.

I am of the descendants of these descendants.

I am not one of the formerly enslaved.

The slave narrative is not a poem.

I wanted to write a cento in which slave narratives centered my experience of being Southern, black, and queer.

I wanted to write a cento in which slave narratives could speak toward my marginal intersecting identities within the South in a way that drew attention to the silences surrounding black life historically that have continued to echo throughout the past two centuries.

The cento creates new meaning.

The slave narrative means that the enslaved and the formerly enslaved recounted their lives from their perspective.

Much of slavery meant denying the enslaved and the formerly enslaved their humanity.

We give narrative to experience every day. Being born and living lawfully in my humanness, I live a reality denied to the enslaved and the formerly enslaved.

Some slave narratives begin, "I was born."

Birth signifies life.

The slave narrative signifies life and testimony. It assumes the lyric position, an act of selfhood and self-possession, upon establishment of the narrative.

In this case, the narrative precedes the lyric.

Being born male and free, I cannot change the meaning of the possessed to fashion a lyric of my own.

This is a matter of ethics. It is a matter of unmaking meaning.

Much of what we know about the lives and times of the enslaved and the formerly enslaved is through a void that is continually being pieced together.

The slave narrative is meant to contribute to closing that void.

Most slave narratives were collected after slavery was officially unlawful.

Many people still did not see the formerly enslaved as people after slavery became unlawful.

This is a true statement: the institution of slavery made the country of the United States into the nation that it is.

This is a true statement: the enslaved and the formerly enslaved built a nation that continued to deny the fact that they were human and not property.

In this case, the slave narrative is a personal account given in spite of the formerly enslaved being denied their humanity.

In this case, the formerly enslaved were continually denied their human right to assume the position of the lyric.

The cento fragments the void, almost already makes the narrative removed, dispossessed again. This is a form of reckoning.

This reverses the meaning of the slave narrative.

The narrative is a device of authority, control.

It is not unlawful to take someone else's voice who had little to no voice preceding their narrative authority.

It is, however, unethical to take someone else's voice who had little to no voice preceding their narrative authority.

This is a matter of ethics.

This is a matter of power.

Some of you reading this have no such ethics, probably because you have a certain amount of power.

In this case, there is power in poetry.

If that is the case, there is power held over and against poetry.

Most of the enslaved were forbidden to learn to read and write.

In this case, the enslaved were forbidden the right to poetry.

Some of the enslaved learned to read and write. Some of the enslaved learned to read and write poetry. In this case, some mastered the lyric in spite of the ways of capitalism.

Again, the lyric is an act of selfhood and self-possession. It should precede narrative.

Again, I must inform you that the enslaved were not considered people socially, politically, economically, or even in the wildest imagination of whites.

The enslaved, the black enslaved, were considered property. They were considered stock.

In this case, could the enslaved fashion the lyric in spite of their subaltern subject position?

Some people are still surprised the enslaved crafted formal lyric in the same way some people are surprised people like me can articulate both word and meaning.

When I say people like me, I mean those descendants of the formerly enslaved.

Again, most slaves were forbidden to learn to read and write.

Some people think it is impossible for me to learn about my ancestors, the enslaved, in spite of—.

We, descendants of the enslaved, have learned to make meaning in spite of—.

Some of you are lost in the poem. This is one form of meaning, meaning I meant for that to happen.

Some of you who are lost know what it's like to be kept out of meaning making.

This is the part where you make your own meaning, ethically.

Some of us can only say what we cannot write.

This is one form of narrative.

This is one form of lyricism.

This is one form of poetry.

If poetry is not testimony, then what is?

If poetry is not a record of the impossible, then what is it?

Sometimes narrative is all we have.

Sometimes narrative is all we are given.

IV

It's what we forget that defines us, and stays in the same place,
And waits to be rediscovered.

—*Charles Wright, "The Southern Cross"*

Tabby

I

I come back,
I come back in dread

to the marsh, to the riverbanks,
to the edge of the sea.

I wade and wait,
swallowed

by the unknowable,
searching the current,

grasping only the void, blurred
vision, receding tides

as I attempt to harvest
what holds history's hollowed

holler in refrain. How could I
come back knowing what I know?

II

It was the wind that howled
the ocean that howled

the belly that rocked
the vessel that spilled

the blood that howled
the night spitting forth

the—, caused her—,
the storm that started

the howl that fed
death so hungry for

the body that wanted
the blood, the bone that sang,

the life that fell
from belly to howling belly.

III

I see them
now, I see them—

opaque waters,
white shell bone

against the dark, just in
time for shucking and sorting,

just in time for crushing
and mixing. I see them

now, I see the bodies,
how they function

against ruin—
tabby hoarding

a vault of them to
this place. I cannot stand

on Sapelo and not hear
the echo of sea. I cannot touch

the walls and not
hear her silence

narrative, feel the weight
of it. I see

the crumbling walls
on Daufuskie, the waves

crashing peril;
I read erasure.

Say *tabby ruins*,
and mean that memory

here isn't made by the makers—
those who turned land and sea

into stone—who endured
times we long to forget.

IV

[the hollow
that was my pain

down there was ruined
cropped a child silent

and stiff so loud loud loud
in memory my memory

for life sent us
into the night

my child still
born into life and

death rocked me
released a sea

into its mouth
the depths of death

for me it was death
that held me]

V

To enter this city is to
confront chaos: past

always looming present
forever facing past,

myth forever a haunting—
Savannah meaning Southern,

Savannah meaning salt,
Savannah meaning river,

the river means to run
the life from me.

Southern as in the bottom,
the bottom of the river,

the river pointing to sea,
the sea meaning salt,

salt meaning cleanse, preserve
the dirty meaning South.

VI

[it was the land that made me
vessel that birthed me

but the sea has given me life
I returned

to the womb
I am alive again

each howl lifts
my body

my belly is the sea
is but salt

another tide
sediment of rock

and viscera
bending shore

from which I holler out
to you

and you and you
becoming you]

VII

Still, memory.
Still.

Almost lost in the beating
of my hands, my arms.

I was lost, back in the mixing
of oceanic flight—the dark

and silent mangled face,
closed mouth when it slid

from her small—no sound.
Her wet—. Her red—.

Leftover matter
in my hands, sounds

still echo in my head.
Still memory.

Again, its spell
at work, bodily possession:

dead baby in the mixing
dead baby in the river

dead baby in the nighttime
standing dead baby

in the trees swinging dead
baby in the roads

dead thing—.
Still. Memory.

And the roaring
current's spirits. Thought I heard

it cry. Swear I saw
her jump from the edge herself.

VIII

Broken. Broken.
Whole. Broken

lodged in sand.
Extend your anxious reach.

Sift. Discover what
you have been given

in shell: voice
of the void.

Hollow to ear—
yield your spirits.

Inside the brittle break-
age—myth.

Infinite depth.
Deep wondrous longing.

IX

These walls, the ground
speak, tell the story

as no one does.
Stone tied to stone—

each crevice a marker
cleaving narrative,

a hieroglyphic of loss.
Each heap of it

pulls the mind astray.
Place your hungry eye

in each split between them,
witness that emptiness

from the outside in
and live there.

Even intervals claim space.
Even intervals monument

what we cannot know.
A shell falls from brick,

even that echo
is a part of me now.

X

I start at the ashore,
(broken, broken)

unsettled
by absence: from Tybee

all down Victory Drive,
I backtrack Sherman's

March to the Sea, past
palm trees lining the road,

through swamp air, thick
ghost of Spanish

moss draped
from the live oak

*(dead baby, dead
baby)* calling out to me.

I go back
to the old city

in honor of the soldier
in Chippewa Square,

his sword drawn in bronze
facing south,

ingrained austere
in my memory *(the blood*

the blood). Honor to
the soldier in Madison Square,

lest we forget
his war

wounds, the bronze
hat filled with bullet shells,

his ever-present
stance over my head.

Honor to the remains
lying in state

over Tomo-Chi-Chi,
those that razed the (*dark*

and silent) native marker.
Honor to the bronze

Bible in Reynolds Square
offered with keen eyes

and a beckoning hand.
I surrender

in Forsyth,
bronze guns and bells

blazoned all around me,
my colonial tongue

confessing: honor (*still
born*) to the Confederate

soldier guarding everything
I must return to—stone

and iron gates forever
denying my lost life

in this city saved
from ruin. I will walk

each step, look up
into him and

XI

[beneath the sea
I did not

become memory
I became echo

density going back
shuttling forth

time and space
land and being

mineral and body
I became soul

of the sea I became
deep center

in the souls of the
living in the deep

beginning
we start with you]

XII

                    pick up
what the South has

anchored. How else
will I outlive it?

I go back
to the river's edge,

back to this waving girl
still in her place,

welcoming
ships to the port—

her white handkerchief
for the returning

and the departed,
finally a flag.

I go back
to the river's edge,

find us in this
one bronze statue

against this many
legacies. I touch

our silent faces,
our eyes cast down and

sideways as birds.
We are not soldiers,

though we fight;
not soldiers,

though we suffer—
we bear no honor.

I will bring my dead
and monument myth.

I will ruin and revise—
I will bring all of the South in me,

the entire wreck
of the nation. In time

I will find my place;
I will return

in tabby, my mouth
full of the sea.

In time I will return
to the river, eyes erect,

facing home, my forward glance—
a defiant waving chain.

Bottom Power

Praise the bottom of USA,
    her blood and sweat in spite of death,
    deep gulf, spinning sea, stretch of moist
    marsh cultured into giving, whose salt
    tears trail into the vast forever and unknown . . .

Praise the plush bottom of USA,
    its tangle of fiber a seat and sanctuary,
    the soft pulled from boll by hard hands,
    afterlife living in the leftover lust of pride . . .

Praise the hard bottom of USA,
    his cane erected willfully in your honor,
    sweet juice on the chin, the return
    each year bent on living, whose seed lives on
    in rich rum-filled romance and rife abandon . . .

Praise the soft bottom of USA,
    her sugar tit still raw with wrought
    of generations, her cotton gin gyration
    inflicted into the games of children
    chattering rhymes on the street corner . . .

Praise the sweet bottom of the South,
    our heft of holler ringing into present
    tense, the lift of fists festered into submission,
    the perverse sway of swamp housing
    the hush of history, the hollow of saltwater
    cyclone seeing and sealing truth, our tapestry
    of tabby toppling over as testimony . . .

Praise the bottom of the black bottom,
    everything lost and lingering, our bone
    of brick still breaking, our emptiness,
    our backward lick of life, our distant

desire, our queer quiet, our will and want,
our silent sighs exalting the cleft clit
still singing in the labor of love . . .

Praise the black bottom of the bottom.
Praise the blackest bottom.
Praise the bottommost black.
Praise the black.
Praise the black.
Praise the bottom.
Praise the bottom.
Praise the bottom.

Notes

Tabby is a type of concrete made of oyster shell, water, lime, sand, and ash. It was used as a substitute for bricks, which were rare and expensive because of the absence of local clay in the Colonial period. The labor-intensive process heavily depended on slave labor and is most common in the Southeastern coastal areas of North Carolina, South Carolina, Georgia, and Florida.

The refrain in "Bop: Black Southern Queer Stories" is taken from "Sissy Man Blues," which was most likely written by Kokomo Arnold of Georgia and recorded by him in the 1930s. Josh White (or Pinewood Tom) of South Carolina also recorded the song. Other acts to incorporate the tune into their repertoire include George Noble and Connie McLean's Rhythm Boys.

"Deep Root" contains an italicized phrase that is taken from Ralph Ellison's *Invisible Man* (1952).

The name "Niggerhead" refers to something that looks like a black person. It was once applied to products such as soap, chewing tobacco, and canned oysters and shrimp. The name has also been used for geographic features such as hills and rocks as well as places, residences, and streets. In 1962, the US Board on Geographic Names changed more than a hundred such names, substituting "Negro." Some names have been changed to include "Colored" instead, with resistance from private landowners. In a 2011 *Washington Post* article discussing politician Rick Perry's family hunting ranch called "Niggerhead," Haskell County Judge David Davis is quoted saying, "It's just a name. Like those are vertical blinds. It's just what it was called. There was no significance other than as a hunting deal."

Index to the American Slave is a book originally published by Donald M. Jacobs in 1981.

It's a common myth that George Washington had dentures made of wood. His estate maintains that he used full and partial dentures composed of materials such as human and probably cow and horse teeth, ivory (possibly elephant), lead-tin alloy, copper alloy (possibly brass), and silver alloy. It is also said that Washington used the human teeth of the enslaved people that he owned. According to Mount Vernon's website:

> Deep within one of Washington's account books is an entry which details Washington's purchase of nine teeth from "Negroes" for 122 shillings. Whether the teeth provided by the Mount Vernon enslaved persons were simply being sold to dentist Dr. Jean-Pierre Le Mayeur or whether they were intended for George Washington, is unknown at this time. Although the fact that Washington paid for the teeth suggests that they were either for his own use or for someone in his family.

Chocolate Plantation is located on the north end of Sapelo Island, a barrier island in McIntosh County, Georgia. One of the Sea Islands, Sapelo is home to descendants of the enslaved who developed the Gullah/Geechee culture and language that have survived into present day. French Royalists occupied the land from 1789 to 1795, naming it "Chocolate" after the Guale Native American village on Sapelo called "Chucalate." Edward Swarbreck bought the land from the French and constructed the tabby main house and slave cabins around 1819. Charles Rogers, owner of Chocolate Plantation in the 1830s, built the tabby barn overlooking Mud River, which was restored by island owner Howard E. Coffin in the 1920s. The main house burned in 1853 during the residency of Randolph Spalding. R. J. Reynolds purchased the island in 1934, and his widow sold it to the state of Georgia, which now manages most of it. The two-story main house had poured tabby walls and chimneys. Some of its walls are poured tabby, while others are tabby brick. Of the outbuildings, the barn, dairy, and smokehouse were tabby construction.

The two italicized lines from "On Stone Mountain" are taken from "My Country, 'Tis of Thee" (Samuel Francis Smith, 1831) and "Dixie" (the anthem of the Confederacy), respectively.

Several lines in "Sugar" are taken from Jean Toomer's *Cane* (1923).

Callie Barr was the longtime caretaker of William Faulkner, who buried her in the same cemetery where he would later lie himself. Her tombstone reads: "MAMMY. Her white children bless her."

Drapetomania was a mental illness said to have caused enslaved blacks to escape captivity. It was later debunked and is now recognized as a type of scientific racism.

The names of the victims and the places of their murders in "1 Yearning" are as follows:

James Webster Smith (West Point, New York)
Unnamed (Madisonville, Texas)
Unnamed (Manatee County, Florida)
Sam Holt (Newnan, Georgia)
Richard Coleman (Maysville, Kentucky)
Will Burts (Columbia, South Carolina)
Louis Rice (Ripley, Texas)
George Ward (Terre Haute, Indiana)
John Pennington (Birmingham, Alabama)
Tom Clark (Corinth, Mississippi)
John Shively (Bloomington, Indiana)
Richard Dickerson (Springfield, Ohio)
Jeff Brown (Cedar Bluff, Mississippi)
Jesse Washington (Waco, Texas)
Bert Smith (Goose Creek / Houston, Texas)
Jim McIlherron (Estill Springs, Tennessee)
Henry Lowry (Millington, Tennessee / Nodena, Arkansas)
Jim Roland (Camilla, Georgia)
"Shap" Curry (Kirvin, Texas)
Mose Jones (Kirvin, Texas)
John Cornish (Kirvin, Texas)
Warren Lewis (New Dacus, Texas)
George Hughes (Sherman, Texas)
George Armwood (Princess Anne, Maryland)
Norman Thibodeaux (Who survived to tell the tale)

"Nocturne: Without Sanctuary" was inspired by *The Wonder Gaze* (*St. James Park, CA. 1935*) (2006–2017) and *Before the Drop* (*c. 1896*) (2013) from Ken Gonzales-Day's *Erased Lynching* series and the exhibition *Shadowlands: Ken Gonzales-Day*, which was on view at the Minnesota Museum of American Art (St. Paul, MN), Flaten Art Museum, St. Olaf College (Northfield, MN), and Peeler Art Center, DePauw University (Greencastle, IN) throughout 2017. In the *Erased Lynching* series, Gonzales-Day removes the tortured body from actual photographs taken during spectacle lynchings. *Without Sanctuary: Lynching Photography in America* (Twins Palms, 1999) is a book by James Allen.

Sullivan's Island, located in the Charleston Harbor in South Carolina, is known as the "Ellis Island of Slavery." Between 1700 and 1775, about 40 percent of enslaved Africans coming to British America (roughly 200,000 to 360,000) came there until the international slave trade was abolished in 1808. A large amount of these enslaved Africans spent time on Sullivan's Island's pest houses, holding cells separating the sick from the healthy until colony officials determined who among them was fit enough for slave auctions. Most African Americans can trace their lineage back to Sullivan's Island.

Acknowledgments

Profound thanks and gratitude to the following publications in which some of these poems first appeared, sometimes in different forms:

The American Poetry Review: "Slave Play," "Self-Portrait as George Washington's Teeth," and "Fucking : A : Proclamation"

Connotation Press: "Niggerhead," "Index to the American Slave," "Niggerhead," and "Drapetomania: Swamp Sublime"

The Georgia Review: "Callie Barr's Black Bottom"

The Iowa Review: "Cento in Which the Narrative Precedes the Lyric"

Los Angeles Review of Books Quarterly Journal: "The Road to Chocolate Plantation"

Tinderbox Poetry Journal: "Power Bottom"

Washington Square Review: "Self-Portrait as an Unmarked Grave," "Addendum"

wildness: "Common Feast"

Yemassee: "A Woman Hangs a Cotton Boll Wreath on Her Door," "Fucking [with] Ralph Ellison," and "Bottom Power"

I owe so much to my family and friends who supported me and these poems before there were poems. You are too many to name. And for that alone, I am forever blessed.

So many thanks to my workshop members from my first two summers at the Cave Canem retreat who welcomed, encouraged, and validated early poems that would eventually define the scope of this project: Alison C. Rollins, Cortney Lamar Charleston, Essence London, George Higgins, Joel Newsome, Kim Marshall, LeRonn Brooks, M'Bilia Meekers, Rico Frederick, Alexa Patrick, Nicholas Goodly, Quenton Baker, Rage Hezekiah, Dave Harris, Mase Johnson, Christopher Rose, and Kush Thompson.

I am forever grateful to have Cave Canem as my first poetry workshop experience and to have shared space with the following faculty, many of whom were some of these poems' first readers: Lyrae Van Clief-Stefanon, Amber Flora Thomas, Kevin Young, Willie Perdomo, Evie Shockley, and Robin Coste Lewis. Many thanks to other Cave Canem staff who shed their light on me those summers: Amanda Johnston, Mahogany L. Browne, Dante Micheaux, Marcus Jackson, and Elizabeth Bryant. Toi Derricotte and Cornelius Eady, infinite thanks for your vision and generosity. Nicole Sealey, thank you for seeing me, your light, and for your fierce leadership. These poems would not be what they are without any of you.

Thank you to my larger-than-life editor, Jeff Shotts, and everyone at Graywolf Press. It has been a decade-long dream to be a part of this family. Thank you for the endless encouragement and for ushering this project and many more into the world with such deep sensitivity, attention, and care.

Immense thanks to the writers I met in Atlanta, Georgia, namely Ryan Jones and the Black Words Collective (Akilah Wise, Kyera Singleton, and Saron Ephraim) who gave me new ways of seeing.

Thank you to S. Erin Batiste, Naomi Extra, Bernard Ferguson, Janee Moses, Brionne Janae, Itiola Jones, Karisma Price, Kwame Opoku-Duku, and Alejandro Perez who read an earlier version of this project and were ready to fight me for almost pulling certain pieces from the collection.

Thank you to Michael Pascual, Cassius Adair, and Sony Coráñez Bolton for their brilliance and whose reading group at the University of Michigan first showed me what a Bottom Studies is and could be.

Thank you to JR Grovner of Sapelo Sights for leading us to Chocolate Plantation on Sapelo Island on my request, even though the rain the day before almost made it too difficult to reach. Immense thanks to Alphonso Brown of Gullah Tours and the staff at the McLeod Plantation Historical Site for sharing so much of the rich history of Charleston, South Carolina.

Thank you to the following professors whose courses trained me to be a literary critic and researcher, and in doing so nurtured my creativity: Monique

Allewaert, Angelika Bammer, Susan (Scotti) Parrish, Michael Awkward, Sandra Gunning, Joshua Miller, Victor Mendoza, Gillian White, Barbara Ladd, Rudolph P. Byrd, Mark Sanders, Lawrence Jackson, and Jonathan Goldberg.

And, finally, profound and unbounded thanks to Chris Abani—one of the most careful readers I know—who saw something in these poems.

MALCOLM TARIQ is a poet and playwright from Savannah, Georgia. He is the author of *Extended Play* (2017), winner of the 2017 Gertrude Press Poetry Chapbook Contest. He has held fellowships from Cave Canem and the Watering Hole. Malcolm was a 2016–2017 playwriting apprentice at Horizon Theatre Company and he was a finalist for the 2018 Princess Grace Fellowship with New Dramatists. A graduate of Emory University, Malcolm has a PhD in English from the University of Michigan. He lives in New York City.

The text of *Heed the Hollow* is set in Vendetta OT.
Book design by Rachel Holscher.
Composition by Bookmobile Design & Digital Publisher Services,
Minneapolis, Minnesota.
Manufactured by Versa Press on acid-free, 30 percent postconsumer wastepaper.